SCHOOLS IN CRISIS

FRAMES
BARNA GROUP

SCHOOLS IN CRISIS
They Need Your Help (Whether You Have Kids or Not)

NICOLE BAKER FULGHAM
RE/FRAME BY KRISTINE SOMERS AND JEFF MARTIN

ZONDERVAN®

ZONDERVAN

Schools in Crisis
Copyright © 2013 by Barna Group

This title is also available as a Zondervan ebook.
Visit www.zondervan.com/ebooks.

This title is also available in a Zondervan audio edition.
Visit www.zondervan.fm.

Requests for information should be addressed to:

Zondervan, *Grand Rapids, Michigan 49530*

ISBN 978-0-310-43322-4 (softcover)

Published in association with the literary agency of The Fedd Agency, Inc,
401 Ranch Road 620 South, Suite 350c, Austin, TX 78734.

Cover design and interior graphics: Amy Duty
Interior design: Kate Mulvaney

Printed in the United States of America

13 14 15 16 17 18 /DCI/ 18 17 16 15 14 13 12 11 10 9 8 7 6 5 4 3 2 1

CONTENTS

WHY YOU NEED FRAMES

These days, you probably find yourself with less time than ever.

Everything seems like it's moving at a faster pace— except your ability to keep up.

Somehow, you are weighed down with more obligations than you have ever had before.

Life feels more complicated. More complex.

If you're like most people, you probably have lots of questions about how to live a life that matters. You feel as though you have more to learn than can possibly be learned. But with smaller chunks of time and more sources of information than ever before, where can you turn for real insight and livable wisdom?

Barna Group has produced this series to examine the complicated issues of life and to help you live more meaningfully. We call it FRAMES—like a good set of eyeglasses that help you see the world more clearly ... or a work of art perfectly hung that invites you to look more closely ... or a building's skeleton, the part that is most essential to its structure.

The FRAMES Season 1 collection provides thoughtful and concise, data-driven and visually appealing insights for anyone who wants a more faith-driven and fulfilling life. In each FRAME we couple new cultural analysis from our team at Barna with an essay from leading voices in the field, providing information and ideas for you to digest in a more easily consumed number of words.

After all, it's a fast-paced world, full of words and images vying for your attention. Most of us have a number of half-read or "read someday" books on our shelves. But each FRAME aims to give you the essential information and real-life application behind one of today's most crucial trends in less than one-quarter the length of most books. These are big ideas in small books— designed so you truly can read less but know more. And the infographics and ideas in this FRAME are intended for share-ability. So read it, then find someone to "frame" with these ideas, and keep the conversation going (see "Share This Frame" on page 84).

Furthermore, each FRAME brings a distinctly Christian point of view to today's trends. In times of uncertainty, people look for guides. And we believe the Christian community is trying to make sense of the dramatic social changes happening around us.

Over the past thirty years, Barna Group has built a reputation as a trusted analyst of religion and culture. We offer cultural discernment for the Christian community by thoughtful analysts who care enough to tell the truth about what's really happening in today's society.

So sit back, but not for long. With FRAMES we invite you to read less and know more.

DAVID KINNAMAN
FRAMES, executive producer
president / Barna Group

ROXANNE STONE
FRAMES, general editor
vice president / Barna Group

Learn more at www.barnaframes.com.

F R A M E S

TITLE	20 and Something	Becoming Home	Fighting for Peace	Greater Expectations
PURPOSE	Have the Time of Your Life (And Figure It All Out Too)	Adoption, Foster Care, and Mentoring – Living Out God's Heart for Orphans	Your Role in a Culture Too Comfortable with Violence	Succeed (and Stay Sane) in an On-Demand, All-Access, Always-On Age
AUTHOR	David H. Kim	Jedd Medefind	Carol Howard Merritt & Tyler Wigg-Stevenson	Claire Diaz-Ortiz
KEY TREND	27% of young adults have clear goals for the next 5 years	62% of Americans believe Christians have a responsibility to adopt	47% of adults say they're less comfortable with violence than 10 years ago	42% of people are unhappy with their work/life balance

PERFECT FOR SMALL GROUP DISCUSSION

FRAMES Season 1: DVD
FRAMES Season 1: The Complete
         Collection

READ LESS.
KNOW MORE.

The Hyperlinked Life	Multi-Careering	Sacred Roots	Schools in Crisis	Wonder Women
Live with Wisdom in an Age of Information Overload	Do Work that Matters at Every Stage of Your Journey	Why Church Still Matters	They Need Your Help (Whether You Have Kids or Not)	Navigating the Challenges of Motherhood, Career, and Identity
Jun Young & David Kinnaman	Bob Goff	Jon Tyson	Nicole Baker Fulgham	Kate Harris
71% of adults admit they're overwhelmed by information	75% of adults are looking for ways to live a more meaningful life	51% of people don't think it's important to attend church	46% of Americans say public schools are worse than 5 years ago	72% of women say they're stressed

#BarnaFrames

www.barnaframes.com

Barna Group

BEFORE YOU READ

....

- When you think of public education today, what are some of the main concerns you have?

- What are some of the major needs of public schools in your area?

- Do you feel equipped to help meet the needs of your local public school?

- How do you think churches should (or shouldn't) get involved in helping public schools?

- Who are some children you know in public schools (besides your own if you have children)? What is their school experience like?

- When you think about reform in public schools, do you feel hopeful or hopeless? Why do you feel that way?

- Would you say helping public schools is a social justice issue for churches? Why or why not?

- In what ways do you think churches could help public schools? Long-term reform? Practical, everyday actions? Prayer and spiritual advocacy?

SCHOOLS IN CRISIS

They Need Your Help (Whether You Have Kids or Not)

INFOGRAPHICS

How are SCHOOLS DOING?

No matter their age, how much money they make, how much education they've had, or what region of the country they live, nearly half of Americans agree—public schools are on the decline.

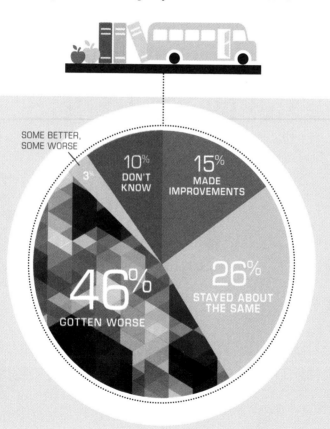

SOME BETTER, SOME WORSE

3%

10% DON'T KNOW

15% MADE IMPROVEMENTS

46% GOTTEN WORSE

26% STAYED ABOUT THE SAME

GRADING SCHOOLS

Teachers get the highest rankings from Americans,
but in general, adults aren't happy
with most aspects of public schools.

*Less than half of Americans have a very
favorable view of public schools*

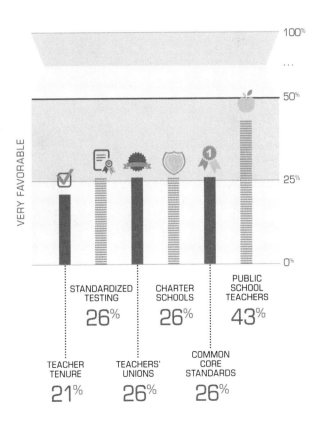

VERY FAVORABLE

100%
...
50%
25%
0%

STANDARDIZED
TESTING
26%

CHARTER
SCHOOLS
26%

PUBLIC
SCHOOL
TEACHERS
43%

TEACHER
TENURE
21%

TEACHERS'
UNIONS
26%

COMMON
CORE
STANDARDS
26%

Should Christians

HELP PUBLIC SCHOOLS?

The answer among practicing Christians is decidedly "yes" (85%). Pastors, in particular, believe it's the place of the church to help with public schools – with nearly all (95%) agreeing.

WHY SHOULD CHRISTIANS GET INVOLVED?

If the vast majority of practicing Christians believe they should get involved in public schools, what is their motivation? Why do they want to help?

1 / It's important to demonstrate Christians' concern for the wider community: **34%**

2 / Part of Christians' responsibility to the poor and needy: **33%**

3 / Public schools are becoming more secular: **19%**

4 / I work in public education or know someone who does: **9%**

5 / Don't know: **4%**

6 / Other: **1%**

"Churches and faith-based groups should be given more opportunities to support local public schools"

77%

Practicing Christians agree

66%

All Americans agree

"Christians should get involved in helping improve public schools"

95%
Pastors agree

85%
Practicing Christians agree

SCHOOLS IN CRISIS

They Need Your Help (Whether You Have Kids or Not)

FRAMEWORK

BY BARNA GROUP

It's a familiar scene: Children skipping to school to start the school year with new clothes, backpacks brimming with supplies, and minds occupied with the question, "What will I be when I grow up?"

But children aren't the only ones mulling over questions about the future. The debate continues over the future of public education in the United States. Everyone has an opinion and (whether or not they realize it) a stake in the outcome — from parents and teachers to politicians and students.

For the last few years, our team at Barna Group has been studying issues related to education. We have been working for various leaders and organizations — some groups are recognizable to the general public, others not as much. This FRAME provides an overview of the challenges and opportunities related to public schools in the United States — giving a survey of the issues, a context for those facts, and a direction to pursue.

"Armchair" Educators

If you follow sports at all, maybe you're familiar with the phrase "armchair quarterbacks." You can picture these folks: sitting at home, away from the hard-hitting action, resting comfortably in their recliners, barking their unsolicited opinions into the ether. At the same time, the players — those literally in the game — are making the actual heat-of-the-moment choices and taking real hits.

Based on the research conducted by Barna Group,

one might conclude we have a nation of "armchair educators," folks who are content to sit back and critique public education but who aren't active in trying to solve the problems.

Just 7% of US adults believe the public education system in the nation is "very effective."

When asked to describe "your ideal world," just one-third of parents of school-age children said they would prefer to send their own children to public schools (34%).

About half of adults (46%) maintain that over the last five years, public schools have further declined. Only 15% of adults say public education has been making progress.

Fewer than 1 in 12 adults are involved in public education as a teacher, administrator (5%), or volunteer (3%).

Armchair educators, indeed.

Yet, we have to admit the entire nation has something to gain by having effective public education. If you're among the more than eight out of ten parents of school-age children who use public schools, you have something to gain. If you're concerned about the quality of the workforce that serves you and the nation in the future, you stand to benefit. If you'd like your community to be healthier and safer, you should care. If you're interested in the economic, social, and—as you'll read in this FRAME—spiritual future of Americans, you have something to gain by helping schools in crisis. And that's not to mention the impact on the lives of the individual students who need a quality education.

Part of what makes for the "armchair educator" problem is that most Americans have opinions about what makes for effective education, and opinions about what should happen in the nation's schools come in a wide variety. Maybe more to the point is that some of us have opinions about what's best for our own children, or the children of those who are close to us, but when it comes to the *other* kids, the "poor minds" who have to attend the lower-performing schools, we tend to be unsure of what to do.

What holds back Americans from helping? The FRAMES research shows the reasons Americans say they feel prevented from being more involved in public school improvement include not having children (47%), not knowing how to help (16%), feeling that education is too political (16%), believing public education does not want religious people to help (14%), thinking schools need more prayer and religious values (12%), doubting they can make a long-term difference (7%), and perceiving that public school culture is contrary to their beliefs (6%).

Whether or not we have children, we all have a responsibility to contribute to the renewal of education. Still, while there may be widespread agreement on the need for reforming education, the pathway to progress is littered with various perspectives on what interventions are best.

Where Faith and
Public Education Intersect

Refining and reforming public education is indisputably a significant challenge. Mobilizing people of faith is certainly among the chief resources that could be integrated into any such efforts. And faith has a significant impact on the contours of the education debate. Here are some examples of how the Christian community plays a part in public education:

Educators — Barna polling shows that nearly half of the nation's public educators are practicing Christians, meaning people who attend church at least monthly and who say their faith is very important in their life. Critics who claim faith has been removed from public schools seem to overlook the countless hours these teachers, counselors, administrators, and coaches devote to educating students.

Volunteers — Additionally, practicing Christians are more likely to volunteer for their local public school than are non-Christians. In fact, of those who regularly volunteer at public schools, two-thirds (65%) attend church. Considering that practicing Christians constitute less than half of the national adult population, their significant involvement in education is statistically exceptional.

Students — More than seven out of ten of the nation's primary and secondary public school students affiliate with Christianity, and millions of those are actively involved in church, confirmation classes, and youth

What matters Most?

Americans name either parents or teachers as the top factor affecting a child's education

51%

Parental support

46%

Quality of teachers

groups. For their part, a majority of today's Christian teenagers expect to complete not only high school but a college degree as well. Interestingly, the pipeline for future educators is strong: 7% of teenagers anticipate being a teacher in the future, a proportion that is strongest among young Catholics.

Parents — The decisions parents make regarding their child's education are clearly some of the most important and personal. For millions of parents in their twenties, thirties, and early forties, their faith and faith community produce a significant influence on their educational choices, preferences, and self-evaluation. Christian parents are influential in the type of schools, colleges, and universities young people attend. Barna research also suggests Christian parents are more self-critical than the norm about their ability to "enable their child to get a good, formal education."

Churches — Many churches in America provide support and volunteers for public schools. For example, almost half of the nation's churches offer support and networking for educators who attend their church. About one-quarter of today's churches offer some kind of mentoring or after-school program for kids or youth. And about two-fifths of youth pastors say they frequently discuss college decisions with students. In churches, families become informed and socialized about issues related to education — sometimes beneficially and sometimes less so. Either way, congregations contribute a great deal to the "educational ecosystem."

The research shows nearly all Protestant pastors (95%) believe Christians should get involved in helping public schools. To a lesser degree, but still significantly, more than eight out of ten churchgoing Christians, regardless of denomination or spiritual devotion, agree Christians should be involved. Exactly how, and for what reason, however, is debated.

For practicing Christians, two reasons for involvement in public education reform stand out: (1) the belief that improving public education is part of Christians' responsibility to help the poor and needy (33%) and (2) the belief that this kind of assistance is important to demonstrate Christian concern for the wider community (34%). Much less important are the worries that public schools are becoming more secular (19%)

"Churches and faith-based groups should be given more opportunities to support local public schools"

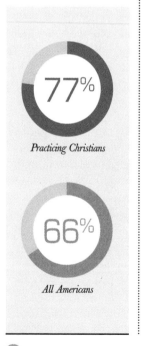

77%

Practicing Christians

66%

All Americans

and working in public education or knowing someone who does (9%).

Comparably, clergy feel showing Christian concern for the community was the top motivation for involvement (40%) and were more likely to say they are inspired by concern that public schools are becoming more secular, with nearly three-tenths holding this view (27%). Also important to clergy is the Christian community's responsibility to help the poor and needy (24%).

Churchgoing Christians believe there are many ways to get involved, with the most popular response for concrete collaboration being to encourage local public school teachers (41%). Other important contributions identified are supporting alternative education options (28%), volunteering at local schools (27%), and working for national reform (26%). Still, only one-third view any involvement as "very important."

Why Write This FRAME?

While we realize public education involves people of a variety of faith perspectives, Barna Group specifically curated this short book with Christians in mind. In this FRAME, we join Nicole Baker Fulgham, president of the Expectations Project, who has a compelling story and point of view on public education. Nicole's experience as a student in Detroit, teacher in Compton and advocate for education in DC gives her a unique and full perspective on education reform. As you'll learn, Nicole is one of those Christians who has moved from the sidelines to the front lines—believing that all children should have an opportunity to have a bright and unlimited future.

Among Christians the research clearly shows there are a variety of opinions about education in general and specifically about public schools. Some Christians are advocates of Christian education or homeschooling. Others believe in the merits of public schooling. And there are differences of opinion between evangelicals, mainline Christians, Catholics, and so on. Opinions as well as the people who hold them are all over the map. Whatever their stance, people ground their views in significant thought, prayer, and belief about what's right for children. There is certainly not a monolithic viewpoint that represents the "Christian" point of view on public education.

This FRAME is not meant to gloss over those differences. Nor is it meant to negate the very personal choices every parent must face about the type of education they think is best for their child. In crafting this FRAME, we do not want to ignore the fact that many Christians have strong opinions and beliefs on this subject.

The factors in the education crisis are complex, and there are no instant or simple solutions. Moreover, it will be difficult to unite various constituencies — all with differing opinions, motivations, and limiting factors — to overcome the significant challenge education reform presents. Regardless, the data suggest practicing Christians are poised to be principal assets in efforts to improve public education.

This FRAME simply takes the facts at face value: We have a nation of armchair educators when many schools — and millions of students — are in crisis. We believe it's time to stop offering unsolicited advice and get in the game. ◆

SCHOOLS IN CRISIS

They Need Your Help (Whether You Have Kids or Not)

THE FRAME

BY NICOLE BAKER FULGHAM

When I was growing up, only two public high schools in Detroit provided a strong, rigorous college preparatory curriculum. I was fortunate enough to attend one of them.

My friend Angie was not.

After I graduated, I began my freshman year at the University of Michigan. In high school, I had worked hard, my parents and my school had prepared me well, and I couldn't wait to become a Michigan Wolverine.

Angie worked just as hard—if not harder.

Angie (not her real name) and I met our freshman year. There weren't a lot of urban African-American students at U of M, and the shared experiences and similar backgrounds formed common bonds among us during our university years.

Angie's high school had a less-than-stellar academic reputation; only half of the students made it through their senior year and earned a diploma. But Angie had quickly risen to the top of her class. She became not only the valedictorian, but one of a select few students from her school to go on to attend a four-year college. Talented, ambitious, and intelligent, Angie was poised and ready to make her mark on our campus.

Like most college students, that initial year was an adjustment for everyone regardless of race, family educational level, or the type of school we attended. Syllabus shock hit us all with full force. Sudden independence, rigorous courses, and the temptation to fill an active social calendar together made for a startling wake-up call. All of us had to adjust to find our way academically.

But Angie, who had graduated at the top in high school, suddenly found herself struggling at the bottom of the incoming freshman class. She had overwhelmingly succeeded at her chronically under-performing public high school, yet now she was floundering in her freshman year of college. How to document sources for a research paper, navigate a heavy reading list with speed-read skills, or apply critical thinking to calculus may have been basic freshman-level skills, but they were entirely foreign to her.

I remember a conversation with her in the quad in the middle of our campus. From all outward appearances, we were standing on common ground, but it soon became clear something else was going on under the surface. There we were—two girls from the same hometown, with the same racial identity, the same freshman courses, the same passion and drive to learn and succeed, and yet my friend felt "different" on a very deep level.

"It's like everyone else is just stepping up a little bit from high school," she lamented. "But I feel like I'm trying to climb Mt. Everest." Her academic struggles were certainly not a result of a lack of trying. In fact, she was more motivated than most students I knew. She enrolled in one of the university's tutoring and academic support programs. Professors knew her by name, since she took advantage of their open office hours regularly. She spent hours in the library and computer lab (yes, these were the days before every student had their own laptop).

The truth is, Angie worked harder than most of us. But it wasn't enough.

"I just didn't realize how much I didn't know," she told me. That conversation in the quad stands out vividly to me because the next year, Angie didn't come back. And she never returned.

Unfortunately, we lost touch, and I don't know the end of her academic story. I'm hopeful she found her way to another school or perhaps even ended up going back to U of M. It was awful to watch someone so gifted and ambitious get slapped with such a brutal life lesson — and during a time when eighteen-year-old college freshmen should be embracing their freedom and determining their life plans. Instead, she came face to face with the knowledge that, while she was a high achiever in high school, she was woefully underprepared for a highly competitive college. And she didn't even see it coming. Talk about feeling conned and cheated.

America's Achievement Gap

Turns out Angie's story isn't uncommon. The *Washington Post* recently ran a story highlighting graduates from historically low-performing public schools in the District of Columbia, and the challenges were the same.[1] Despite tutoring and mentoring support at college, many high school students from urban and rural public schools—even high-performing students— struggle more than the average college freshman. And, like my friend at Michigan, many never graduate. These students thought they were the best and the brightest, but it turns out they aren't even in the same academic league as valedictorians—or even average students, in some cases—from suburban or private high schools.

How did these students end up in these incredibly frustrating circumstances? How can a teenager graduate at the top of their class at an urban public high school but struggle to compete in a basic freshman English class at college? How can a student who received an A in calculus during her senior year of high school get a D in the same subject her first year of college? They worked hard and did all they were told to do in high school. But, apparently, it wasn't enough.

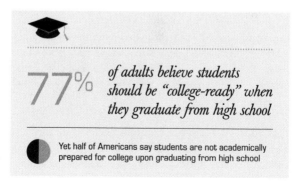

77% *of adults believe students should be "college-ready" when they graduate from high school*

Yet half of Americans say students are not academically prepared for college upon graduating from high school

A Long Way to Go

This kind of inequity is part of what led me to reconsider my own career path.

"What do you want to be when you grow up?" is America's quintessential question for kids. For me, the answer had always been a pediatrician. Of course, I didn't have a particular love for science or math; it just seemed like "the thing to do."

That dream changed as a result of many factors, but one major influence was attending on-campus Bible study classes and talking with the caring pastor who led them. I began to rethink my hopes of becoming a pediatrician (and, if I'm being honest, my sophomore organic chemistry class probably had a little something to do with it too). Through prayer, conversations with professors, and exploring new college courses, I gained enough confidence to rethink my life and my future. I wanted a meaningful career that would have a positive impact on the world. Similar to many American kids, I'd grown up going to church every Sunday, but I came to a point where I wanted to know God for myself and really live my life to honor him. I am forever grateful I came to this realization while I was still in college, and one of my constant prayers was asking God to reveal his purpose for my life.

Back then, I was a student who had made it through Detroit's culture of low expectations and gone to college. Today, I'm the founding president of the Expectations Project, a nonprofit organization mobilizing faith communities to help eliminate education inequity in our public schools. I have no doubt—then and now—that God is working in the public school system to ensure our nation's most disenfranchised children can realize their own potential and purpose.

But we still have a long way to go.

These academic challenges didn't appear overnight. The educational disparities begin long before students graduate from high school. Inequities begin as early as preschool and, if left unchecked, become more severe in middle school and high school.

If you were fortunate enough to attend a strong public or private school as a child, it might be difficult to understand why some students—though bright and capable—can't make it in college. It may seem unconscionable that only 50% of students in low-income communities will ever graduate from high school. And it may seem criminal that only one in fourteen of these young people will ever graduate from college.

After all, isn't America the reigning world power with some of the finest higher education institutions in the world? Immigrants from all over the globe are drawn to our nation, in part, for the illustrious promise of opportunity, equity, and fortune.

Yet, is this an empty illusion? Despite our best efforts to rectify segregation in the 1950s and 1960s, today Native American, Asian-American, black, Latino, and low-income students are still more likely than white, non-Latino students to attend schools where they have little chance of demonstrating academic proficiency, graduating from high school, and attaining the postsecondary credentials that are becoming more and more essential in today's economy. Less than two out of ten black students are enrolled in well-resourced, high-performing schools. Double that amount (42%) attend poorly resourced, low-performing schools. This portrait of imbalance is similar across the board for Native American, Latino, and low-income students. In stark contrast, the average white student is twice as likely to go to a well-resourced, high-performing school.[2]

The disconnect between our educational ideals and the reality of urban and rural low-income public schools is a strong one, yet it plays itself out every day in America.

For most Americans, none of this is particularly surprising. Our FRAMES research shows Americans, at least on a surface level, are aware of this inequality. Yet if your child lives in a safe neighborhood and goes to

More than 4 in 10 black students attend poorly resourced, low-performing schools

Less than 20 percent are enrolled in well-resourced, high-performing schools

Source: The Schott 50 State Report on the Opportunity to Learn in America, The Schott Foundation for Public Education, May 2009

a good school, or if you don't have school-age children at all, you may wonder, "What does all this have to do with me? Of course, the conditions are alarming, but why should I get actively involved?"

Here's why: Because when students aren't able to master basic learning skills, let alone the higher-level critical thinking necessary to compete in our global marketplace, their life prospects are severely diminished.

Our nation's schools in crisis have to do with you and me because the next generation of our nation's doctors, social workers, engineers, teachers, and politicians is sitting in a classroom right now. And if these students are given a substandard education, future generations will be disabled, unable to contribute to society. And as Christians called to champion the image of God in each individual (see Genesis 1:27), to allow these children with incredible potential to fall behind is unacceptable.

So let's examine our nation's education system a bit closer. If we do, we will quickly see what millions of Americans already sense: Our education system is not living up to its promise. In fact, the FRAMES research reveals nearly half of American adults (46%) believe public schools have further declined in the last five years. Only 15% believe the public school system has made improvements.

How do the views of the general population compare with people of faith? Overall, practicing Christians (49%) are slightly more likely than people of no faith (43%) to believe educational quality is in decline. Evangelicals, in particular, carry great concern for the

worsening conditions of the public school system—
two-thirds believe it's in decline.

But if we believe public schools are getting worse, what
can we do to help improve them?

I believe our nation is facing a watershed moment. We
have a choice to make. We have to decide whether we
are going to live up to our promise as the land of equal
opportunity. We must decide whether we will allow our
nation's public education system to continue to prepare
children for one or the other of two very different
futures. And as Christians, America's educational crisis
presents us with a unique opportunity to reflect on
our often ambivalent (and, in some cases, adversarial)
relationship with public schools.

Christians are no stranger to issues of social justice.
We are actively involved in fighting international sex
trafficking, installing clean water wells for remote
villages, sponsoring at-risk children overseas, and
countless other ventures. While such compassionate
action is to be commended, we cannot allow our
perception of justice to be limited to developing
countries. We cannot afford to turn a blind eye on
the educational injustice happening in our cities,
neighborhoods, or within our own families. Not
when the future of the sixteen million kids growing
up in poverty in the US is at stake. Not when quality
education is often what can determine the difference
between a high school dropout unqualified to earn more
than minimum wage and a future contributor to society.
And certainly not when God calls Christians to "Learn
to do right; seek justice. Defend the oppressed" (Isaiah

1:17) and to "defend the rights of the poor and needy" (Proverbs 31:9).

If a quality education is the fundamental pathway out of poverty, then Christians are called to lead the charge in ensuring all young men and women receive excellent educational opportunities. Americans—Christians and otherwise—already know the public school system is broken. But what most of us don't know is what we can do about it.

The immediate impulse, for many, is to simply get their own children out of "the bad schools." When it comes to our own kids, we're often willing to go to great lengths to secure a proper education—whether that's choosing to homeschool, paying the expenses to put kids through private school, moving to a new school district, or enrolling children in lotteries in the hope they will be one of the lucky few who find a better quality option in their own neighborhood.

While these options may be good ones for some families, they are not options for millions of families in our nation—particularly for those in poorer neighborhoods. What can these parents and families do to get a high-quality education for their children? Who will speak up for these children?

This conundrum is precisely why Christians need to work together to improve the public school system. Our schools are in crisis—and the future generations of doctors, scientists, social workers, teachers, entrepreneurs, and more are in crisis as a result.

WHAT TO DO?

Americans aren't happy with
their public schools, that
much is clear.

*So what do Americans think will improve
lower-performing schools?*

1 / Greater family and parental involvement: **76%**

2 / More high-quality teachers: **70%**

3 / Increased funding: **48%**

4 / Rigorous, consistent academic standards: **45%**

5 / More involvement by faith communities: **35%**

6 / Vouchers: **31%**

7 / Charter schools: **24%**

The good news is that we can work together to do something about it.

Educate Early and Often

Not too long ago I was meeting with a group of pastors in a Midwestern city. We came together for a daylong discussion about how we can work together to help improve educational opportunities for children in some of their city's poorest neighborhoods. We eventually zeroed in on the lack of public preschools as a major root cause of disadvantaging kids early on. Their state is one of the few left in the entire country that doesn't provide any public funding for preschool.

One by one, the pastors shared stories about the challenges families in their congregations face. These challenges echoed a common theme: Many of the family's struggles began before their children even reached elementary school. Single parents couldn't find adequate child care, so relatives or friends ended up watching their little ones during the day. Two-parent families struggled to make ends meet with low-wage jobs, and the private preschool options were far beyond their financial means. Many of the churches had day care centers in their facilities as a much-needed resource for struggling families.

While pastors were pleased they'd found a way to support these parents, they knew their limited financial resources often meant their day care centers weren't able to provide all they hoped for these future students. As one of the clergy noted, "It's tough when you know your little ones will compete with suburban kids whose parents can afford to pay $15,000 or $20,000 a year for the Rolls Royce of preschools!"

Another pastor told a different story. Their church's preschool program was an incredible success. Nearly every child in the class, most of whom were from low-income African-American families, were reading at a kindergarten level by the time they graduated out of the program.

"What an astounding testimony to God-given potential inherent in all children," I thought. "What a phenomenal example showing academic disparity doesn't have to exist."

"However," the pastor continued, "when we send our babies on to the local public elementary schools in our neighborhood, they end up falling academically far behind once they're in second or third grade." He described the heartbreak these families and the church with them felt in watching their preschoolers' remarkable progress erased in their elementary years.

Maintaining Educational Equity

If there is disparity in preschool, surely the situation only becomes graver in elementary and middle school.

As a fifth grade teacher, my first school was in Compton, California, an urban community near South Central Los Angeles. My students showed so much potential: They were intellectually curious young people who loved learning about ocean creatures and the California gold rush. My girls and boys delighted in decoding logic puzzles and math problems. They enjoyed reading—diving into adventure books and working in groups to illustrate the story's plot, theme, and characters.

Yet the majority—more than two-thirds—were at least two to three grade levels behind the standards for fifth graders statewide. Many students were reading and performing math skills at the level of a second grader or below.

Why? It's not because my fifth graders were held back once or even twice, as many assume. No, these children had made it through the school system without learning to read at grade level. And this is where the public schools often fail their students. On paper, none of my fifth graders had officially failed the previous grade. Yet cognitively, they had failed to master the material from one year to the next and were left with critical knowledge gaps.

Unfortunately, my elementary classes in California are not unique. On a national level, most children from low-income communities are already three grade levels behind their peers in wealthier communities by the time they reach fourth grade.[3]

That's three years' worth of learning. And when three years is a third of a child's young lifetime, it sets them back immeasurably. Just look at how this trend is

Students from low-income communities are three grade levels behind their peers in wealthier communities by the time they reach fourth grade

Students who aren't proficient readers by third grade are four times more likely to drop out of high school

Sources: U.S. Department of Education (2007) and *Double Jeopardy* by Donald Hernandez

linked to high school dropout rates: Studies show that students who aren't proficient readers by third grade are *four* times more likely to drop out of high school.[4] Elementary school is truly a make-or-break time for many children—and not just for their childhood and young adulthood but for the rest of their lives.

The High School Dilemma

As one might imagine, the middle school and high school years don't get any better for children who have fallen behind academically in earlier grades. Low-income students are five times more likely to drop out of high school than their higher income counterparts.[5] And of those who do graduate, many will end up like my friend Angie—arriving at college incredibly capable, committed to getting ahead, but woefully academically unprepared.

It's a widespread national problem. But let's take a look at one city, Indianapolis, to illustrate how high schools end up allowing students who don't have a firm grasp on the material to graduate in the first place.

Several years ago, the state of Indiana passed a bill allowing for a small number of high school students in each district to receive their diplomas despite having failed the state's basic graduation tests in reading and math (a standard ninth grade Algebra 1 exam and a tenth grade English test). These waivers were intended to be given out judiciously, and only in extreme circumstances.

While only 8% of graduating seniors received "waiver diplomas" across the state at large, several state districts began to graduate large percentages of high school students via these waivers. The majority of Indiana's school districts with a high percentage of waivers also have extremely high minority and low-income populations. In Indianapolis, for example, 27% of the graduating seniors received waiver diplomas. This rate was even higher among African-American students, 30% of which received waivers. This percentage of black students who used a district-approved waiver is not only strikingly high, it is disproportionate even when compared with other demographic groups educators identify as at risk. For example, one in seven Indiana students who received free and reduced-price school meals—a standard measure of poverty—received waivers. For Hispanic students, the rate was also one in seven. Yet black students were consistently awarded these waivers the most.

Needless to say, parents and local and state leaders were outraged when these practices came to light.[6]

We Sink or Swim Together

So that brings us to an uncomfortable question: Why should we care that millions of children in public schools don't have access to a high-quality education? If our children's schools are fine, or we don't even have school-age children, why should we be concerned about schools in crisis?

Human nature tempts us to turn a blind eye to suffering that isn't right in front of us. Perhaps it's some type of unconscious emotional self-preservation; perhaps our hearts can only tolerate a certain amount of tragedy and despair. I don't know. But I do know I'm guilty of this on a regular basis. I cannot count the number of times I've seen shocking footage of a natural or human-caused tragedy on the national news and, being a crier to the core, grabbed the Kleenex and wiped my eyes for the next few minutes. Sometimes, that immediate emotional reaction is followed up with a quick Google search to learn more. And even less often, I might send a donation to the Red Cross later that day.

But if I'm honest, I have to admit that my most common reaction is to forget about whatever drove me to tears just hours or even minutes before. Sure, I may think about it again occasionally. But the creature comforts of my life afford the privilege of being lulled back into complacency relatively quickly.

I remember the first time our youngest daughter noticed a homeless person on the street in downtown Washington, DC She was about three years old. We passed an older gentleman sleeping on the sidewalk, with his possessions close by in a shopping cart. My daughter walked by wide-eyed. I could tell she was trying to formulate a verbal response. So I waited. A couple of blocks later she questioned, "Mommy, why was that man taking a nap on the street?" I gently explained to her that he probably didn't have a home. Incredulous, she asked countless follow-up questions. We talked about homeless shelters, what it must be like to sleep outside when it's cold or snowing, and whether or not he had children of his own.

Unlike my teary-then-forgotten encounters with the hard things in life, this was an experience that stayed with my daughter, an experience she took to heart. For months, our preschooler returned to the topic of the homeless man. He became a permanent fixture in her nighttime prayers. Weeks would go by and she would ask me if I thought he was able to find a job and get a house by now. Months later we were in the same neighborhood, and she wanted to try to find him. Our daughter was aware she had a cozy bed full of stuffed animals and soft pillows inside her warm home with Mommy, Daddy, and her siblings, but she was also suddenly aware not everyone lived as she did.

Can you imagine what would happen if we didn't just pass by the injustice of the public schools' broken system? If we lived in the simple recognition, like my daughter did, that not everyone lives as we do? If instead of passing by and getting back to a life of comfort, we took on the role of the Good Samaritan in Luke 10 and helped our neighbors? Because the truth is, there is no "us" and "them" in God's calling of Christians to care for their neighbors. We are all neighbors together—and together, in our country's educational crisis, we will sink or swim.

As if God's call to love our neighbors isn't reason enough, I believe there are three compelling reasons why the church must make it our mission to heal the broken public school system.

Purpose-Driven Schools

Our nation's schools in crisis is a looming social injustice—putting millions of children, their families, and their future families at stake. It is also a political injustice, and it requires political reform to enable public schools to be the best they can be. But there is another injustice in our schools today—a spiritual injustice.

As Christians, we operate in the conviction that everyone is created for a unique God-given purpose. And I suspect most of us agree a child's education can play a significant role in helping to unlock that purpose. Common sense dictates if a child demonstrates strong potential to become a physician or a journalist, for example, the quality of their schooling is directly proportional to the likelihood of achieving that purpose. Conversely, a substandard education limits that child's contributions to society.

The bottom line is this: The brokenness in our

educational system is not only a social injustice; it is a spiritual injustice, with the power to severely hinder God's purpose for millions of children.

I know what you may be thinking. How can we possibly ascertain God's purpose for millions of children growing in poverty? And isn't God big enough to find a way to help all children—regardless of background—have a fruitful and fulfilling life? I'm not a theologian, so I don't have all the answers to those questions. On one level, I have no doubt God's plans are much deeper than my or your finite brain can conceive, so I fully believe he can redeem inequities and lost opportunities. He clearly does this every day! But I also deeply believe we have a problem when we live in a nation where certain groups of children graduate with incredibly strong foundations while others don't graduate or graduate without needed skills.

It's even more unjust when those two groups of children are generally divided by race and family income. The Bible lays out a framework for understanding God's compassion and commitment to the socially disadvantaged, which becomes our mission as well. Proverbs 31:8–9 proclaims for God's people to "Speak up for those who cannot speak for themselves, for the rights of all who are destitute. Speak up and judge fairly; defend the rights of the poor and needy." In contrast, those who deliver injustice to society are clearly outside God's favor, as Isaiah 10:1–2 says, "Woe to those who make unjust laws, to those who issue oppressive decrees, to deprive the poor of their rights."

A Literate People

As an extension of our conviction that all people are created with divine purpose, the church should have an inherent interest in seeing children achieve their full potential. A big part of this — and a big part of our faith as well — is literacy.

Literacy not only influences one's ability to thrive in school, follow an intentional career path, and engage the world, but influences the extent to which future generations will understand our religious traditions and pass them on to their own children.

Literacy affects every aspect of a person's life. And, as Christians, we should care deeply about the kind of life people are being equipped to lead. But, as Christians, literacy resonates with us at an even deeper, spiritual level as well. We are a community that centers itself on a book of truth, so literacy is essential for spiritual education. Think about what church would look like if no one could read: There would be no Scripture reading from the pulpit, no library of theological resources, no children's ministry curriculum. Pastors wouldn't be able to prepare a sermon without the ability to consult commentaries or even the Scripture passage itself. Worship song lyrics on a screen or in a hymnbook would be meaningless without anyone being able to understand them. Even if church leaders could rely solely on memory and oral teachings to deliver spiritual truth, congregants wouldn't be able to verify their teachings or go deeper into them for themselves.

An illiterate church is hard to imagine in today's world,

44%

OF ALL ADULTS SAY

"It is extremely important to me that my children attend college"

Practicing Christians	51%
Other faith	41%
No faith	36%

Black	61%
Hispanic	64%
White	38%

Less than high school	41%
High school grad / some college	43%
College grad or more	53%

Less than $40K	41%
$40K - $60K	43%
More than $60K	52%

yet some people are facing a life of illiteracy. The result is a social, perhaps even spiritual, disability. The ability to read has vast implications for life and faith. The degree to which individuals are literate, educated, and able to think critically directly impacts the level of engagement in a congregation. And the better the education young people receive the greater likelihood they will contribute and participate in society in meaningful ways.

It's About the Economy

The education crisis is felt deeply by the single mom who can't afford to send her kids to a private school, the parents who have no choice but to send their son off every day to high school troubled with violence, and the child who has dreams of becoming a violinist but with no public resources that enable her to follow that dream.

The impact of our schools in crisis is felt deeply at an individual level. But its effects don't stop at an individual or a family. Poor education has a ripple effect that extends to the community, the nation, and the world.

Let's look at the economics of the achievement gap between student demographics. An undereducated population profoundly impacts our nation's productivity and global competitiveness today. The facts are clear:

- If the United States had closed the gap between its educational achievement levels and those of better-performing nations such as Finland and Korea, GDP in 2008 could have been $1.3 trillion to $2.3 trillion higher. This represents 9 to 16% of GDP.

- If the gap between black and Latino student performance and white student performance had been similarly narrowed, GDP in 2008 would have been between $310 billion and $525 billion higher, or 2 to 4% of GDP.

- If the gap between low-income students and the rest had been similarly narrowed, GDP in 2008 would have been $400 billion to $670 billion higher, or 3 to 5% of GDP.[7]

For these reasons—helping all children reach their God-given purpose, ensuring we have a literate nation of critical thinkers, and securing the future economic stability of our country—public educational inequity impacts all of us.

My Brother and Sister's Keeper

Raise Your Voice for Public Educational Equity

Even though evangelicals believe our nation's public schools are headed in the wrong direction, many of us are conflicted about how we should engage this problem—and if we should even engage it at all.

Among Christians, the most common response to the problem is a personal solution to the public school crisis. An overwhelming majority of Christians would prefer to send their children to private religious schools if given the opportunity.

Only 6% of Americans who attend church regularly send their children to religious schools, but 47% say they would prefer to send their children to religious schools if they could, followed by a combined 28% who would choose homeschooling, private schools, or charter schools. Conversely, while 84% of churchgoing parents send their children to public schools, only 24% say that is their first choice.

These gaps between parental preferences and reality are massive. In comparison, 40% of people who don't attend church regularly say public schools are their first choice.

If we people of faith so strongly prefer to send our own children to religious schools, why aren't we equally as motivated to help improve the very public schools we perceive are failing?

I believe it is because we struggle to reconcile two seemingly conflicting ideas: (1) America's public schools are woefully underserving our nation's most disenfranchised children, so Christians should help improve them, and (2) we Christians overwhelmingly wish we didn't have to send our own children to public schools (although most of us do).

What is surprising is that Christians already have an overwhelming presence in the public schools — they are disproportionately represented among public school

IDEAL *versus* REALITY

Most American parents – Christian or not – currently send their kids to public schools. However, not many of them are happy about it. In an ideal world, many Americans would choose another option.

Public schools

Currently use:

Churchgoing Christians	84%
All Americans	85%

Ideal choice:

	24%
	34%

Private secular schools

Currently use:

	2%
	3%

Ideal choice:

	11%
	19%

Private religious schools

Currently use:

	6%
	8%

Ideal choice:

	47%
	31%

Charter schools

Currently use:

	6%
	4%

Ideal choice:

	9%
	7%

Homeschool

Currently use:

	9%
	6%

Ideal choice:

	8%
	9%

*Percentages may not add up to 100% due to multiple children per household and rounding.

employees. They are teachers, coaches, principals, and superintendents, and they are already actively involved in the lives of our nation's children.

Strategically placed, deeply aware of the problem, and grounded in a faith that calls us to uphold justice and empower the human dignity and purpose of all, it would seem Christians are poised to influence our schools for the better. So why aren't we?

I'm going to make a huge leap, although hopefully an instructive one, to further explore this idea:

During the 1980s and 1990s, the AIDS crisis rocketed into an international epidemic. Millions of new cases were reported annually, and the world got front-row seats to one of the worst humanitarian crises of our time as news media broadcast the epidemic and its effects far and wide.

Yet the evangelical church was initially reluctant to reach out to communities devastated by HIV/AIDS. There was a tacit, and in some cases extremely verbal, stance that reflected the cultural wars of the times.[8] Some evangelical leaders pushed the idea that AIDS was a punishment from God dished out for homosexuals, fornicators, and drug users. The disease's social taboo made many evangelical Christians squeamish in offering their support.

Fast forward a decade or two, and we see a completely different picture. The national evangelical community has shifted their stance dramatically during the last ten to fifteen years, and today Christian leaders and organizations are some of the biggest supporters of HIV/AIDS prevention and follow-up care around the globe. The National Association of Evangelicals, World Vision, Willow Creek Community Church, and Saddleback Church, among many other Christian organizations, have truly become leaders in responding to this major health crisis.

What lessons can we draw from this example? I will be the first to admit using this analogy runs the risk of hyperbole. Men, women, and children dying from a debilitating disease represent an altogether different kind of pain than children who are left behind in woefully under-performing public schools. However, I believe we can take away several key insights from the comparison.

First, the Christian community's understanding of *why* a major social issue exists can deeply impact our willingness to engage it. In the case of HIV/AIDS, the conventional wisdom, at least until the last decade or so, was that people infected with HIV were more to be blamed than to be helped. The underlying logic was, "If you don't want AIDS, don't have sex outside of marriage." Within this framework, it's much easier for a larger church community to absolve itself of responsibility—to simply walk away from problems perceived as a result of poor moral choices rather than operate with an ethic of caring for our brothers and sisters—regardless of how or why they contracted a life-altering disease.

Within the context of the public school debate, perhaps a similar attitude is at play on several levels. Christians, who most often hold the traditional family structure in high esteem, might not view educational inequity as an issue that connects to them. When someone is less familiar with a community, it's easy to fall into believing stereotypes about the challenges they may face. And so we often entertain stereotypes about low-income parents, single moms, or parents who themselves aren't educated. Simply put, our perceptions about the moral factors impacting public education may inadvertently cause some Christians to judge families who attend low-performing schools. And that judgment, whether conscious or subconscious, may give us the sense that we're somehow off the hook to find a solution to the problems.

Layered into this absolution of responsibility is another factor. If, as the above data suggests, we Christians don't believe public schools are the best place for our own children, why would we feel a responsibility to improve them? Complicating this further, many of our churches see helping our schools as a *parental* responsibility rather than a *spiritual* responsibility. When surveyed, 85% of Christians cited increased parental involvement as the number one factor in improving student achievement in low-performing schools (as compared to 76% of general population). Christians ranked high-quality teaching next highest at 74% (compared to 70% of general population). No other factors received above 60%. The bottom line? Christians understand public educational improvement as a responsibility of parents rather than the responsibility of all Christians as local school community members. In fact, nearly half of all regular churchgoers (44%) say the main factor that holds them

WHO IS RESPONSIBLE?

When it comes to children's education,
Americans generally feel the responsibility
should be shared between parents and
schools, though they tend to believe
parents play a slightly larger role.

*Primary
responsibility for
educating children
rests with*

56%

School system

80%

Parents

*Most important
factor for
a student's
education*

47%

Teachers

51%

Parents

*Factors for
improving student
achievement in
low-performing
schools*

70%

*Recruiting high-
quality teachers*

76%

*More parental
support*

back from helping local public schools is because they don't have school-age children.

I completely understand this reasoning. Problems become more real when you or your loved ones are personally affected. But let's play out this line of reasoning for a moment. If those without school-age children take themselves out of the equation, then that leaves only people with children. Yet millions of privileged and middle-class families with school-age children send their kids to private schools or to better-performing public schools with no academic inequities. So that would leave only the parents of the fifteen million children growing up in poverty to fight against the inequality and substandard schools in many of their neighborhoods.

Having been raised in urban Detroit myself, I completely believe in the potential of self-empowerment and a local community's demand for change. That said, breaking out of the cyclical nature of generational poverty is much more challenging for families and individuals without institutional help. But, oh, the strength that can be harnessed when other communities join alongside them to collectively meet their needs! My parents, who both came of age as African-Americans during the civil rights movement, marveled at the visceral power of white men and women joining African-American civil rights leaders to integrate bus lines, diners, and swimming pools.

Invoking shared Christian responsibility to combat challenges has another practical implication that may or may not directly affect our personal world. Communities that have been historically disenfranchised can benefit from people with additional political, financial, and social capital. Those assets add increased resources to aid in the community's struggle. And the benefits go both ways: People with more resources can learn much from families in more economically challenging communities.

I submit, when people of faith are at our best, we answer God's call to help those afflicted by injustice even when we have no apparent skin in the game. It is then that we beautifully and lovingly model the biblical idea of being our brother and sister's keeper. It is then, as we learn to share one another's burdens, that we stand shoulder to shoulder and begin to embrace the pain and suffering others face. As Dr. King eloquently stated in his *Letter from Birmingham City Jail*: "Injustice anywhere is a threat to justice everywhere."[9] We are in this together.

Do Public Schools Want "Christian" Help?

My husband and I recently attended a dinner party hosted by friends who are involved in philanthropic efforts with public schools. As I explained some of my work, one guest expressed surprise at my efforts, which include intersecting faith and public education. The guest held the common opinion that separation of church and state means faith and public education cannot coexist. Having heard this objection before, I spoke from my own perspective as a former public school teacher and the immense involvement my church had as tutors and mentors in my classroom. I mentioned the fact that, according to our research, while four out of five churchgoing Christians believe churches should help public schools, one in five say they don't think public schools actually *want* their help.

To my delight, one of the other dinner guests, who works in the area of religious freedom issues, then backed me up. He surprised us all by sharing with us the numbers of religious student groups that exist in public schools. While the popular narrative suggests religious help isn't welcome in public schools, the last twenty years or so have seen a marked increase in after-school religious programs such as Young Life or Fellowship of Christian Athletes. Our perceptions of Christian help not being appreciated may be hindering us from helping where it is needed most. But the truth is, our help is very much wanted.

In the World ... But Not of It

One recent afternoon, I had just settled in for a radio interview with a Christian station. Radio interviews are one of my favorite things to do, partly because it gives me the opportunity to speak to an audience about what I believe are important issues, and partly (let's be honest) because it's all audio so I can do the interview in my sweatpants. As always, I was excited to talk about the work we're doing with the Expectations Project, which builds advocates for public educational equity within faith communities.

WAYS THE CHURCH CAN HELP

1 / 36%
Encouraging teachers

2 / 25%
Supporting alternative education options

3 / 24%
Volunteering at local schools

4 / 24%
Working for national education reform

5 / 22%
Working with the local school board for reform

6 / 19%
Helping local schools with fund-raising

WHAT'S HOLDING US BACK?

1 / 44%
I don't have children in public school

2 / 18%
I don't think public schools want religious people to help

3 / 18%
Education is too political

4 / 17%
I'm unsure how to help

5 / 16%
Schools need more prayer and religious values, not academic support

6 / 9%
Public school culture is contrary to religious beliefs

*Among churchgoing adults

**Percentages equal more than 100 because respondents could choose more than one answer

About midway through the interview I was asked a provocative question: "Wouldn't Christians be better served by putting their money, time, and resources into creating schools that align with our own Christian values and beliefs?"

This wasn't the first time I'd heard this general line of thinking. In fact, according to our FRAMES research 78% of practicing Christians believe there is not enough teaching on character and values in public schools and only 40% would agree the morality and values taught in public schools support their faith. But perhaps because I was on the air, or because of the sincerity with which the question was asked, it struck a chord in me that day. Because my work is primarily with public schools, I'll admit I sometimes develop tunnel vision. And I absolutely believe opening and offering faith-based schools has incredible merit.

But here's what ultimately brings me back to focusing on the public education system: The vast majority of children in our nation attend public schools—well over 90%. The realist in me believes that, at least for the foreseeable future, most kids in our country will attend public schools. And that's where the biggest inequities exist. Therefore, public schools represent the biggest opportunity for Christians to make an impact on a massive societal injustice.

I don't think there's anything wrong with opening Christian schools that provide all children with the opportunity to receive both a high-quality academic education *and* Christian values—far from it. Growing up in Detroit, I attended a parochial elementary school that was relatively affordable for our working-class family. And it was great!

But unfortunately, even my modest Christian school option was financially far out of reach for almost all of my friends and neighbors. Given the financial obstacle that parochial schools present, I caution my fellow brothers and sisters in Christ against viewing Christian schools as the *only* way to solve the academic disparities in our country. I believe we have to be realistic about where the biggest challenges exist and focus a disproportionate amount of our efforts there. Right now, those biggest challenges exist in our nation's lowest-performing public schools.

When I started the Expectations Project, a close friend told me we wouldn't really have arrived until people publicly started disagreeing with us and pushing back against our ideas. Sure enough, as soon as we dipped our toes into social media, the games began. And as we have expanded our reach, the Expectations Project has received candid pushback from some Christians who believe that, as a faith-based organization, we should be explicitly sharing our faith with children in public schools.

One of our team members, Blythe, kept me in the loop about one particularly loquacious commenter on our blog who repeatedly encouraged us to shift our mission so we were explicitly sharing Christ with children in the schools. Otherwise, this individual argued, all of our work to help improve academic outcomes would be in vain. Or, as another blogger put it, writing from the voice of public school students, "You helped improve our schools, but we're going to hell!"

It's a fairly small number of Christians who express this concern—in our research only 16% of churchgoing Christians said schools need more prayer and religious values, not academic support—but this minority is often a vocal minority. So, after much discussion, Blythe crafted a response, not so much to debate but to help our team wrestle through this complex issue. Here's what Blythe helped us articulate as an organization:

> We believe God put us in the world not to remove ourselves from it, get saved, and wait for heaven, living in fear our children will be corrupted by the world. Rather, he commanded us to be "salt and light" in the world ... We do not believe [Christ] would want us living in fear of the world, judging it while refusing to enter in and help change it, as he did! Christ commands us to love *all*, and desires everyone knows the full life he desires for them on this earth now. A full life in Christ means eternal life, yes, but it also means having the opportunity to live to our full potential, having a chance to live the life he desires for us while we are on this earth. By being present in our public schools, through our words and our actions, we are being salt and light. We are showing the love of Christ.

It's an interesting conundrum, isn't it? I think anyone who engages in faith-motivated advocacy has to wrestle with how forthcoming to be with one's religious beliefs. I err on the side of letting our actions and compassion speak for themselves. Quite simply, I know we wouldn't be able to work with public schools if we didn't respect two things: (1) the law and (2) the individual religious (or non-religious) beliefs of every teacher, administrator, parent, and child in the public school system. And for me, that's where the conversation begins and ends.

Respecting these boundaries doesn't mean we don't pray daily for the children and families in urban and rural public schools. We do—with great joy and anticipation! One of my most fulfilling moments was when the Expectations Project team collectively crafted prayer points to share with faith communities in our network.

We've already discussed the three reasons many Christians hold back in getting involved with public schools: because they don't feel accountable to be their brother and sister's keeper, because they wonder if public schools truly want their help, and because they believe public schools don't share their values. We often discuss each reason as though it is a strictly black-and-white, either/or decision. But I encourage you to push your thinking beyond these unhelpful dichotomies.

As Christians wrestling with massive societal inequities, the issues are much more nuanced than we like to believe. We don't have to pick between starting Christian schools or helping public schools. We don't need to choose between sending our children to religious schools or helping families and schools in low-income communities. We are a diverse community of believers who can simultaneously work in different methods for the common good. By identifying the deep inequities at work and doing what we are each uniquely fitted to do, we can collectively help solve this massive problem in our nation.

Advocacy Vs. Action

As the Expectations Project has helped faith communities get into the nitty-gritty of how they can help public schools, one of the push/pulls we often feel is the tension between getting involved locally versus participating in long-term advocacy.

I've long believed part of the power of the church is our passion around "heart" issues: We see a need and we want to solve it. It's truly a beautiful thing to behold! I believe it has led to thousands of congregations doing great work for schools, including donating classroom supplies, launching feeding programs for students who come to school hungry, building new playground equipment, and painting dull, paint-chipped school walls.

However, where this heart passion often seems to evade people of faith is in a concerted effort to work on long-term systemic issues that influence our public schools. Issues like universal preschool, viable avenues to recruit and retain high-quality public school teachers, and effective data management systems don't have the immediate "feel good" impact that feeding a classroom full of hungry students offers. Given that, one might believe people of faith will never want to go more in-depth on systemic institutional issues impacting our nation's public schools. Surprisingly, this couldn't be further from the truth. FRAMES data reveals that,

LONG-TERM REFORM

56% *"I would prefer to work for long-term education reform"*

66%
Schools need broad reform more than immediate assistance

30%
I feel more effective at working for long-term reform

21%
Long-term reform is a better reflection of my religious views

7%
Trying to help with immediate needs is too complicated

VS.

44% *"I would prefer to help local public schools in practical ways"*

60%
Schools need help now, not just down the road

41%
I feel more effective at helping in practical ways than advocating for reform

26%
Educational reform is too political

11%
Practical assistance is a better reflection of my religious values

PRACTICAL AND IMMEDIATE HELP

*Among churchgoing Christians
**Percentages equal more than 100 because respondents could choose more than one answer

between institutional reform and local immediate action, 56% of churchgoing Christians would rather work on long-term systemic reform compared to 44% who want to help public schools in what they consider more "practical, everyday ways." The good news is that there are opportunities for both.

Civility and Racial Reconciliation

As in addressing any problem, one of the first steps is to get people talking. However, this can be more challenging than it seems at first. It has been said that religion and politics aren't fit topics for polite company, and if you have ever attended a public education debate, you might shy away from that topic as well. These debates can certainly get heated. Everyone brings their own perspective and persuasive tactics. Special interest groups can overtake the dialogue, leaving others to feel they must dig in their heels even further. And for those of us who recognize common ground on both sides, it's difficult to carve out a nuanced space that feels authentic.

To further complicate things, the people whose lives are affected by our subject of debate are rarely there to represent themselves. Many people from historically disenfranchised communities (particularly lower-income African-American and Latino populations) often report feeling left out of the discussion altogether. The debate is handed over to community leaders, educators, or whoever's talking the loudest. Frankly, the "solution" often takes the face of the white privileged convening in a room, but the door often appears shut to the families who are most deeply affected. Not surprisingly, this dynamic leaves many affected by the education crisis feeling more excluded than empowered.

I don't want to oversimplify the role of faith communities in bringing civil discourse and helping with racial reconciliation within education issues. The frustration runs deep across many communities, and the issues are real. But I am hopeful if we enter these conversations with a different perspective, then we may be able to make some inroads. Christian communities themselves are incredibly diverse, and many African-American and Latino faith leaders are already actively engaged in local education issues. If we do this work respectfully and carefully, I believe we have the opportunity to create a different type of positive discourse within the public square—one in which all are welcome.

Prophetic Servant Leadership

The problem is, admittedly, immense. And as with most systemic issues, there aren't any quick fixes. There isn't a magic "it" factor that will suddenly cause thousands of under-performing schools to turn around. Instead, it requires hard, steady, passionate, committed, relentless effort. As a member of this ever-growing movement of people who are not willing to allow the academic achievement gap to continue, I find it necessary to hold fast to faith and hope.

And hope, even now, is already beginning to take root. We can look to the growing number of examples of

How did the church HELP YOU?

There are a variety of ways churches can get involved in helping students with their education: mentoring, scholarships, college counseling. But when asked, very few 20- to 29-year-old Christians said their church had helped them with their education.

3% Received a scholarship for college through church

3% Learned about schools/colleges through church

12% Received helpful input from a pastor/church worker about their education

16% Had an adult mentor at church other than pastor/ staff

classrooms and schools that are truly defying the odds. These schools are no longer glamorized, Hollywood-esque exceptions to the rule. In neighborhoods where crime and poverty far exceed the national average, children are graduating and attending colleges *at the same rate* as suburban students. The Urban Prep Academy, an all-boys public school on the south side of Chicago, sends 100% of its African-American senior class to college every year. Jefferson Middle School, a public school in Washington, DC, saw students' standardized test scores increase by double-digit margins. Their students even outpaced the test score gains of schools in wealthier communities! These examples, and the hundreds like them, remind us of what our kids can do — if given the opportunity.

And that's where we put our hope into action.

We must ask ourselves, how do we replicate these successes in schools around the country? Why are those schools and classrooms working where others struggle?

Research suggests incorporating the following best practices can help close the academic achievement gap:

- Raising and maintaining high expectations for all students,

- Supporting and developing highly effective teachers,

- Creating a positive and achievement-oriented classroom culture, and

- Extending the school day or school year so children have more time to learn.[10]

But what about the church? How can Christians get involved—even Christians who don't have school-age children or don't already work in the school system? Here are some ways we can lend our efforts (and check out The Expectations Project's website for additional resources):

- Volunteer one hour a week to tutor children in lower-performing public schools.

- Host small group discussions at your church to increase awareness about educational inequity.

- Start a partnership with a public school by asking the

school leadership how your church can best make a difference.

- Become aware of education issues impacting schools in your community and reach out to local, state, or federal decision makers to learn how you can help.

Four out of five churchgoing Christians already believe churches should help public schools—and 95% of their pastors agree with them. More than one-third of regular church attendees believe churches can help improve schools by actively supporting local district and school board leadership or partnering with local public schools to help support them. We already have the numbers, so let's get moving.

We have the opportunity to join the prophetic voices of other generations who have worked on behalf of the most disenfranchised communities. We can lift up a vision of what's possible for children in low-income communities to achieve in schools. There's a reason the story of my friend Angie's taking the fall from

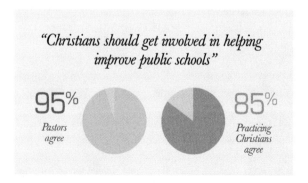

"*Christians should get involved in helping improve public schools*"

95% Pastors agree

85% Practicing Christians agree

high school valedictorian to college dropout pricks our conscience. There's a reason we feel uncomfortable when faced with the reality of parents who have no alternative options to a low-performing public school for their kids.

Social injustice should always provoke us in this way. Let it provoke us into action. Because for as many heartbreaking stories there are of how public schools have failed our nation's children, I believe there is also room for stories of hope. Hebrews 11:1 reminds us, "Now faith is confidence in what we hope for and assurance about what we do not see."

I wrestle with questions of the unseen every day: How will each of us hold on to the idea of educational excellence for all public school children, even though we do not yet see that in every urban and rural classroom? How will we share that vision within our own faith communities? Beyond merely hoping for a different education system, in what ways is God tugging at our hearts to take action and be a part of the solution?

Millions of children in low-income communities are waiting to hear our answers. ◆

SCHOOLS IN CRISIS

They Need Your Help (Whether You Have Kids or Not)

RE/FRAME

BY KRISTINE SOMERS AND JEFF MARTIN

Roosevelt High School is one of the most ethnically diverse high schools in Oregon with one of the highest percentages of poverty-stricken students. Nearly 85% of its kids qualify for free or subsidized lunches. One out of eight students is homeless. Even the school itself is tired-looking, with peeling paint, graffiti-tagged walls, and weeds surrounding the main doors.

SouthLake Church wanted to help. We approached a school administer to tell him our congregation wanted to offer student mentoring, and his response taught us a crucial lesson in what kind of help public schools really need. After quietly listening to our grand scheme, he replied, "Thank you, but I should tell you that's a little like proposing marriage before the first date."

Roosevelt may have needed our support, but we needed to earn their trust first. We quickly learned that when it comes to faith-based support of public schools, *how* we support them matters.

That was five years ago, and we've come a long way since in partnering with Roosevelt High School. Along the way, we've identified three guiding principles churches can adopt to pave the way for a successful, long-term partnership with public schools.

1. Leave Your Agenda Behind

Through our work with BeUndivided, a nationwide organization supporting church involvement with public schools, we often tell those who want to help that the best way to convince people you don't have an agenda is to not have an agenda. Don't come with an objective. Come to serve—in any way you're needed. In other words, come to love as Jesus did.

For SouthLake Church, love came in the form of thousands of volunteers gardening, painting, window-washing, and repairing. Then it took the form of clothing, feeding, coaching, and mentoring Roosevelt's students. And then it took fund-raising and strategizing on an institutional level.

This kind of love takes work. Yet the clear absence of an agenda tied to proselytizing was key to our ability to establish and maintain a meaningful relationship with Roosevelt High School. Before long, no one seemed to be asking about SouthLake's agenda. They stopped asking, "Why are they here?" And instead they started suggesting, "Maybe SouthLake will help."

2. Serve with Humility

Charlene Williams, the principal of Roosevelt High School, has a PhD in education and more than fifteen years of experience. Like the other educators at the school, she is an expert in the field of education, and yet she is overwhelmed as she stands in front of any given classroom in her school. Not because of a lack of expertise, but because of a lack of resources. Charlene and her colleagues are overwhelmed because of the incredible obstacles to education that so many of their students carry with them into the classroom—poverty, homelessness, learning disabilities, hunger, neglect, abuse. There are simply not enough resources — human or financial — to help all of those kids through their obstacles.

For a church entering into this kind of environment, the best approach is one of humility. Let's be honest: We don't really have "the answer" to America's public education crisis. What we *do* have is a willingness to be part of the solution. And that is more than enough.

Recognizing that principals, teachers, and other educators are already doing the extraordinary, we don't need to show up with well-laid plans for school reform. All we need to do is ask one question that Jesus modeled for us in Mark 10:51: "What do you want me to do for you?" This question communicates clearly, "*You* are the expert on the needs of your school. We are simply here to serve."

A pastor in Florida recently told us he approached the principal of his neighborhood elementary school with this very question. The principal, expecting to hear a program pitch, was floored. "No one has ever just offered to *help* us before!" he said. We think there is no better place for such an offer to come from than Christ's church.

3. Exceed Expectations

One of our mantras for serving at Roosevelt is "Under promise and over deliver." We learned the reason for this the hard way. In our enthusiasm to get involved early on, we committed to launching a coaching-support program that we ultimately did not have the bandwidth to implement. Fortunately for us, our school contacts were forgiving despite the disappointment. We learned, however, that especially in an environment of great need, the strong temptation is to say "yes" to every request. But when a "yes" now turns into a failure to deliver later, it can erode the very trust you've been trying to build.

As representatives of Jesus, we have to model who he is by being people of our word and doing what we say we're going to do. It is important for churches to begin a supportive partnership with a public school by focusing on only one or two service projects church leaders are certain they can deliver. We best honor those we serve when we exceed the expectations we've set for them. That being said, it's also important to be people who know how to say "I apologize" when we've fallen short.

With these three principles as guides, we believe successful long-term church and school partnerships can thrive and even transform communities.

Here are a few practical steps to get you started:

Five First Steps for Church and School Partnerships

- Meet with a local school principal. Without bringing your own expectations, ask for three or more suggested ways in which your church could help.

- Meet with your team to discuss and identify one of the principal's suggestions your church could implement with excellence.

- Identify a gifted leader to serve as point person to lead the new outreach to the school.

- Communicate the vision to the church and recruit the resources and volunteers needed.

- Visit www.BeUndivided.com for additional resources and help. ◆

....

Kristine Somers *led the establishment of the SouthLake/ Roosevelt partnership and is cofounder and program director for BeUndivided—a Portland-based organization created to inspire and equip churches to serve in public schools across America.*

Jeff Martin *is cofounder and national partnerships director for BeUndivided and producer of the highly acclaimed film* Undivided. *Jeff owns and operates It Matters, a media solutions company based in Oregon.*

AFTER YOU READ

- Now that you've read, do you think it's important for Christians to engage with public schools? If so, why?

- Look up state or local ratings to identify schools in your area that are struggling. If you feel called to help, talk with a few people at your church about ways to engage with one of those schools using some of the practical ideas in this FRAME.

- Do you know any public school teachers or employees at your church? Talk with them in the next few weeks and ask them how you can support them. One thing you can certainly do is pray regularly for them.

- What are your thoughts on "not having an agenda" when it comes to helping with public schools—especially when it comes to evangelizing?

- When it comes to schools in crisis, what compels you to want to help? Having kids in school? Protecting the future of our society? Breaking cycles of poverty? Something else?

- What are two or three ways you can begin helping public schools in your area in the next few months? This could be anything from praying for teachers you know, to signing up at a local mentoring center, to coordinating a group of volunteers at your church to engage a local public school as SouthLake Church did.

SHARE THIS FRAME

Who else needs to know about this trend?
Here are some tools to engage with others.

SHARE THE BOOK
- Any one of your friends can sample a FRAME for FREE.
  Visit zondervan.com/ShareFrames to learn how.

- Know a ministry, church, or small group that would benefit
  from reading this FRAME? Contact your favorite bookseller, or
  visit Zondervan.com/buyframes for bulk purchasing information.

SHARE THE VIDEOS
- See videos for all 9 FRAMES on barnaframes.com and use
  the share links to post them on your social networks and share
  them with friends.

SHARE ON FACEBOOK
- Like facebook.com/barnaframes and be the first to see new
  videos, discounts, and updates from the Barna FRAMES team.

SHARE ON TWITTER
- Start following @barnaframes and stay current with the
  trends that are influencing and changing our culture.

- Join the conversation and include #barnaframes whenever
  you post a FRAMES related idea or culture-shaping trend.

SHARE ON INSTAGRAM
- Follow instagram.com/barnaframes for sharable visual
  posts and infographics that will keep you in the know.

Barna Group   ▰ ZONDERVAN®

ABOUT THE RESEARCH

....

FRAMES started with the idea that people need simple, clear ideas to live more meaningful lives in the midst of increasingly complex times. To help make sense of culture, each FRAME includes major public opinion studies conducted by Barna Group.

If you're into the details, the research behind the *Schools in Crisis* FRAME included 1,086 surveys conducted among a representative sample of adults over the age of 18 living in the United States. The survey was conducted from May 10, 2013, through May 20, 2013. An additional telephone survey included 1062 interviews conducted among a representative sample of adults, 18 years of age and older, from within the 48 continental states. The survey included 331 cell phone interviews. The survey was conducted from April 13, 2012, through April 18, 2012. The sampling error for both studies is plus or minus 3 percentage points, at the 95% confidence level.

If you're really into the research details, find more at www.barnaframes.com.

ABOUT BARNA GROUP

In its thirty-year history, Barna Group has conducted more than one million interviews over the course of hundreds of studies and has become a go-to source for insights about faith and culture. Currently led by David Kinnaman, Barna Group's vision is to provide people with credible knowledge and clear thinking, enabling them to navigate a complex and changing culture. The company was started by George and Nancy Barna in 1984.

Barna Group has worked with thousands of businesses, nonprofit organizations, and churches across the country, including many Protestant and Catholic congregations and denominations. Some of its clients have included the American Bible Society, CARE, Compassion, Easter Seals, Habitat for Humanity, NBC Universal, the Salvation Army, Walden Media, the ONE Campaign, SONY, Thrivent, US AID, and World Vision.

The firm's studies are frequently used in sermons and talks. And its public opinion research is often quoted in major media outlets, such as *CNN, USA Today*, the *Wall Street Journal*, Fox News, *Chicago Tribune*, the *Huffington Post,* the *New York Times*, *Dallas Morning News*, and the *Los Angeles Times*.

Learn more about Barna Group at www.barna.org.

THANKS

Even small books take enormous efforts.

First, thanks go to Nicole Baker Fulgham for her passionate work on this FRAME — offering her years of devotion and hard-earned lessons in the public school system to create what we pray is a prophetic and practical challenge to the church and to Christians, whether they have kids
or not.

We are also incredibly grateful for the contributions of Kristine Somers and Jeff Martin, who, along with their team at BeUndivided, have led the way in thoughtful church and public school partnerships.

Next, Barna Group gratefully acknowledges the efforts of the team at HarperCollins Christian Publishing, especially Chip Brown and Melinda Bouma for catching the vision from the get-go. Others at HarperCollins who have made huge contributions include Jennifer Keller, Kate Mulvaney, Mark Sheeres, and Shari Vanden Berg.

The FRAMES team at Barna Group consists of Elaina Buffon, Bill Denzel, Traci Hochmuth, Pam Jacob, Clint Jenkin, Robert Jewe, David Kinnaman, Jill Kinnaman, Elaine Klautzsch, Stephanie Smith, and Roxanne Stone. Bill and Stephanie consistently made magic out of thin air. Clint and Traci brought the research to life—along with thoughtful analysis from Ken Chitwood. And Roxanne deserves massive credit as a shaping force on FRAMES. Amy Duty did heroic work on FRAMES designs, from cover to infographics.

Finally, others who have had a huge role in bringing FRAMES to life include Brad Abare, Justin Bell, Jean Bloom, Patrick Dodd, Grant England, Esther Fedorkevich, Josh Franer, Jane Haradine, Aly Hawkins, Kelly Hughes, Steve McBeth, Geof Morin, Jesse Oxford, Beth Shagene, and Santino Stoner.

Many thanks!

NOTES

1. Emma Brown, "Graduates from Low-performing DC Schools Face Tough College Road," *Washingtton Post*, June 16, 2013, http://www.washingtonpost.com/local/education/graduates-from -low-performing-dc-schools-face-tough-college-road/2013/06/16/ e4c769a0-d49a-11e2-a73e-826d299ff459_story.html.

2. "The Schott 50 State Report on the Opportunity to Learn in America," The Schott Foundation for Public Education, May 2009, 7 – 9.

3. "National Assessment of Educational Progress (NAEP) Reading Assessment," U.S. Department of Education, Institute of Education Sciences, National Center for Education Statistics, 2007.

4. Donald Hernandez, *Double Jeopardy: How third grade reading skills and poverty influence high school graduation,* Annie E. Casey Foundation, April 2011.

5. "Trends in High School Completion and Drop Out Rates in the United States: 1972 – 2009," U.S. Department of Education, Institute of Education Sciences, National Center for Education Statistics, October 2011.

6. Scott Elliot, "Waivers allow graduation for nearly 27% in IPS who failed stated test," *Indianapolis Star*, June 1, 2012, http:// www.indystar.com/article/20120630/NEWS04/207010353/ Waivers-allow-graduation-nearly-27-IPS-who-failed-state-tests.

7. The Economic Impact of The Achievement Gap in America's Schools, McKinsey&Company, April 2009, 5 – 6.

8. Chan Woon Shin, "Are Culture Wars Over? U.S. Evangelicals and the Global AIDS Crisis," Syracuse University, Religion, Media & International Affairs, http://sites.maxwell.syr.edu/luce/ChanWoong.html.

9. Martin Luther King Jr., *Letter from Birmingham City Jail* published in *Why We Can't Wait* (Harper and Row: 1964).

10. Nicole Baker Fulgham, *Educating All God's Children: What Christians can — and should — do to improve public education for low-income kids*, (Grand Rapids, MI: Brazos Press, 2013), 189 – 199.

Share Your Thoughts

With the Author: Your comments will be forwarded to
the author when you send them to *zauthor@zondervan.com*.

With Zondervan: Submit your review of this book
by writing to *zreview@zondervan.com*.

Free Online Resources at
www.zondervan.com

Daily Bible Verses and Devotions: Enrich your life with daily
Bible verses or devotions that help you start every morning
focused on God. Visit www.zondervan.com/newsletters.

Free Email Publications: Sign up for newsletters on Christian
living, academic resources, church ministry, fiction, children's
resources, and more. Visit www.zondervan.com/newsletters.

Zondervan Bible Search: Find and compare Bible passages in
a variety of translations at www.zondervanbiblesearch.com.

Other Benefits: Register to receive online benefits like
coupons and special offers, or to participate in research.